EXPLORING OUR SOLAR SYSTEM

THE SUN

DAVID JEFFERIS

Crabtree

DANGER
NEVER look at the Sun directly. Its rays are strong enough to cause permanent damage or blindness to unprotected eyes.

■ OUR LOCAL STAR

The Earth and other planets revolve around our nearest star, the Sun. The energy in sunlight supports almost all life on Earth. Without the Sun's heat, the Earth would be a frozen snowball. Its warmth is also the power that drives the ecological systems on our planet, giving us our climate, weather, and ocean currents.

The Sun's rays can also be dangerous. Too much of the Sun's rays can damage crops, cause droughts, sunburn, or skin disease.

Crabtree Publishing Company
PMB 16A,
350 Fifth Avenue, Suite 3308
New York, NY 10118

616 Welland Avenue,
St. Catharines, Ontario
L2M 5V6

Editors: Ellen Rodger,
Adrianna Morganelli

Published by Crabtree Publishing
Company © 2008

Written and produced by:
David Jefferis/Buzz Books

Educational advisor:
Julie Stapleton

Science advisor:
Mat Irvine FBIS

■ ACKNOWLEDGEMENTS
We wish to thank all those people who have helped to create this publication. Information and images were supplied by:

Alpha Archive
Jeff Bryant
ESA European Space Agency
Goddard Space Flight Center
iStockphoto:
Brown Dog Studios
Matthew Cole
Stephen Inglis
Manfred Konrad
JAXA Japanese Space Agency
JPL Jet Propulsion Laboratory
Kitt Peak National Observatory
NASA Space Agency
Gavin Page, Design Shop
Solar Kankeo
Snr Airman Joshua Strang, US Air Force (aurora picture)
UKSSDC UK Solar System Data Centre
Certain pictures courtesy of: HAO/SMM C/P project team and NASA.
HAO is a division of the National Center for Atmospheric Research, which is supported by the National Science Foundation.

Library and Archives Canada Cataloguing in Publication

Jefferis, David   The sun : our local star / David Jefferis.

(Exploring our solar system) Includes index.
ISBN 978-0-7787-3733-9 (bound).
--ISBN 978-0-7787-3749-0 (pbk.)

    1. Sun--Juvenile literature. I. Title. II. Series: Exploring our solar system (St. Catharines, Ont.)

QB521.5.J44 2008   j523.7   C2008-901218-6

Library of Congress Cataloging-in-Publication Data

Jefferis, David.
   The sun : our local star / David Jefferis.
       p. cm. -- (Exploring our solar system)
   Includes index.
   ISBN-13: 978-0-7787-3749-0 (pbk. : alk. paper)
   ISBN-10: 0-7787-3749-7 (pbk. : alk. paper)
   ISBN-13: 978-0-7787-3733-9 (reinforced library binding : alk. paper)
   ISBN-10: 0-7787-3733-0 (reinforced library binding : alk. paper)
   1. Sun--Juvenile literature. I. Title. II. Series.

   QB521.5.J44 2008
   523.7--dc22
                                    2008006377

■CONTENTS

■WHAT IS THE SUN?

The Sun is a star. It's a huge ball of super hot, glowing gases, 860,000 miles (1.4 million km) across — that's 109 times wider than Earth!

WOW!
Compared to Earth, the Sun is BIG! The little blue dot below (arrowed) shows the Earth to scale with the Sun at right.

This large arch of gas is called a **prominence**

■ The surface of the Sun glows at a temperature of more than 9,930°F (5,500°C). Inside the Sun, temperatures are thought to be millions of times hotter than this.

Flares explode off the surface

■ IS THE SUN BIGGER THAN OTHER STARS?

The Sun only looks bigger because it is closer to us than any other star. In fact, as space distances go, the Sun is just "next door" to Earth — the next closest star is trillions of miles away! There are many stars that are bigger or smaller than the Sun. It is about average for brightness, size, and temperature.

The surface is called the **photosphere**

■ This picture shows what our galaxy looks like. We are located toward the edge (arrowed). The Milky Way is just one galaxy among countless others.

■ WHERE IS THE SUN?

The Sun belongs to a huge, slowly turning spiral of stars, called the **Milky Way galaxy**. The Milky Way is made up of more than 200 billion stars, and our Sun is just one of them. Earth is located far away from the heart of the Milky Way.

5 ■

■ HOW OLD IS THE SUN?

Most scientists believe the Sun formed about 4.6 billion years ago. Its birthplace was in a vast cloud of gas and dust in space, called a nebula.

■ HOW DID THE SUN FORM?

In the middle of that nebula, dusty gases swirled around like cream in a cup of coffee. As time went on, parts of the mixture came together in dense blobs. These blobs gradually became bigger and hotter, until they began to glow, lighting up the nebula with starlight. The star we call the Sun came from this nebula.

WOW!
Stars form in distant gas and dust clouds called "star nurseries." The Orion nebula is the most active "nursery" we know of.

□ Nebulas come in all shapes and sizes. Here in the Orion nebula, young stars shine through misty veils of gas and dust.

WILL THE SUN ALWAYS LOOK THE SAME?

Most definitely not! When it was young, the Sun was smaller and hotter than it is now.

In about 5 to 6 billion years, the Sun will run out of its **hydrogen** gas fuel. When this happens, changes inside the Sun will cause it to expand, to form a bloated "**red giant**", hundreds of times bigger than the Sun is today.

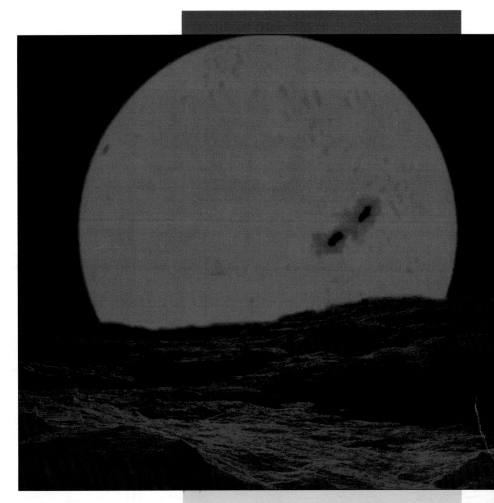

■ Sunrise could look like this when the Sun becomes a red giant. By then, the extra heat will have blasted away the Earth's air, seas, and oceans. If any humans survive at this time, they will have escaped to other planets.

WILL THE SUN BLOW UP IN THE DISTANT FUTURE?

The Sun will not end its days as a red giant. In the far future, its outer layers will rip apart to form a cloud (left). A small hot core, called a **white dwarf**, will remain. When this eventually cools down, only a dark cinder, called a black dwarf, will survive.

■WHAT IS THE SOLAR SYSTEM?

The solar system **is our local group of planets and moons, including Earth, that** orbit **the Sun.**

Neptune

Uranus

Saturn

Jupiter

■ Here the eight main planets are lined up according to size. There are also a number of smaller, dwarf planets, such as Pluto and Ceres.

■ WHERE DID THE PLANETS COME FROM?

Most scientists think the planets formed from the same gas cloud as the Sun. The planets are all very different, but they fall into two main groups.

The four planets nearest the Sun are smaller, and have solid surfaces. They are called "rocky worlds." The four outer planets are much bigger than the rocky worlds. They are called "gas giants" because they are made mostly of gases, and do not have any kind of solid surface.

WOW!
The Sun is the biggest object in the solar system. It contains about 99 percent of all matter.

■ WHAT ARE THE BIGGEST AND SMALLEST PLANETS?

The largest of the planets is mighty Jupiter. It is made mostly of hydrogen and **helium** gases, that swirl in vast, cloudy bands. The only feature that has remained the same over the years is the Great Red Spot. This is a huge storm that has raged for more than 300 years. It is big enough to swallow the Earth several times over.

Mercury is the smallest planet, and the the one closest to the Sun. It has no air, is hot enough to melt lead, and is peppered all over with craters.

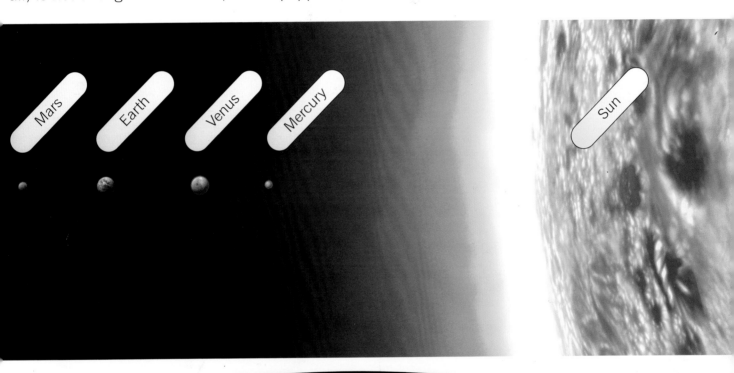

■ Each planet goes around the Sun in a near-circular path called an orbit. It takes the Earth 365 days to complete an orbit, a period we call a year. Other planets make longer or shorter orbits.

■ WHAT IS THE SUN MADE OF?

The Sun is a giant ball of gas. It is 71 percent hydrogen gas and 27 percent helium gas. The other two percent is a mixture of other gases.

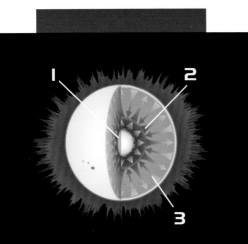

■ **There are three main layers that lie deep inside the Sun:**
1 **Core**
2 **Radiative zone**
3 **Convective zone**

■ HOW DOES THE SUN SHINE?

The secret of the Sun's power lies in its center, or **core**. Core temperatures reach more than 27 million° F (15 million° C). Under these extreme conditions of heat and pressure, a special kind of burning happens: **nuclear fusion**. In nuclear fusion, particles of hydrogen join together, or fuse, to make helium. As they do this, energy is given off, and it is this mighty power that provides the Sun's heat and light.

■ WHAT HAPPENS TO THE CORE'S ENERGY?

Energy from the Sun's super hot core gradually makes its way to the surface, at first moving through the **radiative zone**. Further out, it heats layers of gas in the **convective zone**. These turn over in a surging motion, much like water in a boiling saucepan. Finally, energy reaches the surface of the Sun, the photosphere, where it escapes into space.

■ IS THE SUN MAGNETIC?

Yes! The swirling gases deep inside the Sun create powerful electric and **magnetic fields**. This process also creates huge magnetic loops, sometimes up to 500,000 miles (800,000 km) high.

■ **Much of our recent knowledge about the Sun comes from space laboratories, such as the SOH space probe, shown here against an artist's idea of the Sun's interior.**
SOHO, which stands for Solar and Heliospheric Observatory, was launched in 1995 by a United States/European science team, and still in working order.
SOHO is 932,000 miles (1.5 million km) from Earth. It carries a dozen instruments to study the Sun.

WOW!
Energy from the Sun's core travels outward very slowly. It takes thousands of years to finally reach the outer, or convective, zone.

■DOES THE SUN SPIN?

Yes it does, though the Sun takes longer to rotate than Earth's 24 hours. The Sun makes a complete turn just once in about 25 Earth days.

■ WHAT IS THE SUN'S SURFACE CALLED?

The visible surface of the Sun is the photosphere, but like the rest of the Sun, it is not solid. The photosphere is in constant motion, with streams of super hot gases rising and falling through the convective zone just below.

WOW!
Granulations are fast moving and do not last long. Each granule lasts only up to 20 minutes, before sinking back under the surface.

■ DO OTHER STARS HAVE PHOTOSPHERES?

Yes, it's a general word used for the glowing surface of any star, big or small. However, the Sun's photosphere is the only one we can study closely – other stars are too far away to see anything in detail.

▣ **Tracking the progress of a feature across the Sun (marked above by the blue arrows) allows scientists to check how fast it rotates.**

The pictures show the movement of a huge surface explosion called a flare. This flare lasted for just over two weeks before fading away.

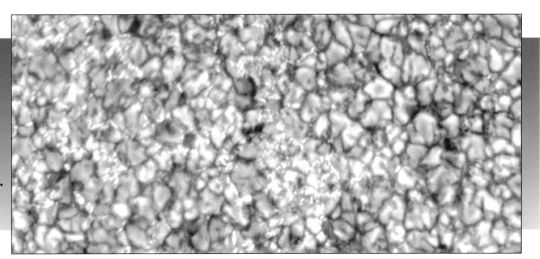

■ This telescope view shows the bubbling look of granulations. Each granule is about 600 miles (1,000 km) across.

■ WHAT ARE GRANULES?

If you look closely at the photosphere, you can see that it has a moving pattern, called granulation. The granules are caused by the bubbling up-and-down movements of gases from below the photosphere.

■ ...AND SUPERGRANULES?

Granules also form bigger patterns across the whole of the photosphere. These are called supergranules, as shown in this computerized image.

WHO FIRST SAW A SUNSPOT?

Sunspots are magnetic storms in the photosphere. The first likely sightings were made by Chinese astronomers, more than 2,200 years ago.

■ HOW BIG ARE SUNSPOTS?

Sunspots look like small dark specks on the Sun. However, they are not really small at all. Even a medium-sized sunspot may be several times wider than the Earth.

Sunspots often appear in groups, which grow over a period, then gradually fade away again.

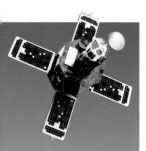

■ The TRACE satellite has taken many pictures of sunspots.

■ WHERE DO SUNSPOTS APPEAR?

Sunspots appear where the Sun's magnetic field breaks through the surface. Then the boiling granulations are forced back, outside the sunspot area.

Sunspots are magnetic and usually occur in pairs, linked by an invisible magnetic loop. After a few days, weeks or months, the magnetism fades, and so do the sunspots.

More than 100 sunspots may appear during a busy year

Umbra

Granulations

Penumbra

■ WHY IS A
SUNSPOT DARK?

It looks dark because it is cooler
than regions nearby, about
7,200° F (4,000° C), instead of 9,930° F (5,500° C).

■ WHAT IS THE UMBRA?

This is the very dark central part of a sunspot. It is named after the
Latin word for "shade." Surrounding a sunspot's **umbra** is a lighter
area, called the penumbra.

WOW!
Sunspots had
been seen for many
years, but it was not
until the year 1612 that
the astronomer Galileo
explained what
they were.

WHAT IS A SOLAR CYCLE?

The solar cycle **is a period of about 11 years during which all solar activity, including sunspots and prominences, reaches a peak then dies away again.**

SolarMax
satellite

WHAT IS SOLAR MAX?

It's a short name for the peak of sunspot activity. It was also an astronomy satellite that was launched in 1980.

1997

1998

These pictures show the Sun as it approached the solar maximum of 2000, from a fairly quiet star to an energy powerhouse.

Solar maximum is important to us because the electronic equipment used by satellites for radio, TV, and telephones can be damaged or knocked out completely by a powerful burst of solar energy.

HOW MANY SUNSPOTS ARE THERE?

Solar cycles are all slightly different, so it's impossible to predict the exact number of sunspots in any particular year. There have also been long periods when few sunspots appeared at all.

WHO DISCOVERED THE SOLAR CYCLE?

It was the German astronomer Samuel Schwabe, in 1843.

WOW!
Strange things happen to the Sun's magnetic poles at solar maximum, when they do a flip-flop – the North and South poles swap over!

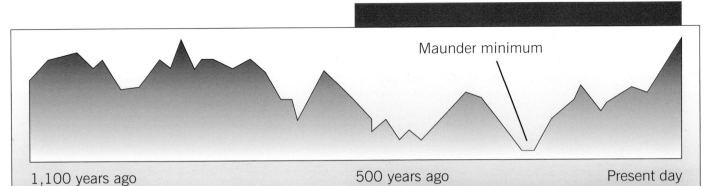

1,100 years ago   500 years ago   Present day

Maunder minimum

■ **This chart shows the rise and fall of sunspot numbers over the centuries. Very few sunspots were seen in the years from 1645 to 1715. It's a period called the** Maunder Minimum**, named after the English astronomer Edward Maunder, who first noticed the link between sunspot numbers and Earth's climate.**

■ **Early paintings show what happened when sunspots disappeared for long periods. This icy winter scene was painted in the year 1410, during such a cold spell.**

1999

■ WHAT WAS THE LITTLE ICE AGE?

For reasons that are not fully understood, the Earth's climate can be affected in times of little sunspot activity, and winters can be far colder than usual.

The "Little Ice Age" was a time when rivers and lakes, even parts of the seas, froze solid for months at a time. The Little Ice Age lasted on and off for six centuries, from about the year 1250 to 1850.

■ IS A PROMINENCE BIG?

Prominences are huge eruptions of gas that extend from the surface of the Sun out into space.

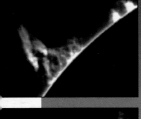

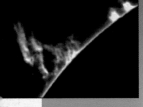

■ These pictures show the progress of a prominence. Each shot was taken at intervals of about 15 minutes. It might not look impressive until you realise that at this scale, the Earth is no bigger than the tiny globe shown below.

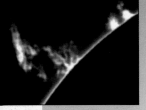

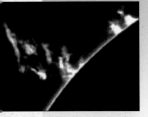

■ HOW BIG IS A PROMINENCE?

One of the biggest prominences was seen in 1997. It stretched across 219,000 miles (350,000 km), a distance more than 27 times wider than the Earth!

■ WHAT DOES IT CONTAIN?

Compared with the air we breathe, the gases that make up a prominence are very thin. Even so, because it is so huge, a prominence may contain about 100 billion tonnes of material.

■ These four pictures were taken by the SOHO space probe (see page 10). The hottest areas appear white in these computerized images, cooler areas in red.

Prominences are made of gases in the form of a plasma – which is much like a far hotter version of the ultra-thin gas in a home fluorescent light tube. Twisted magnetic fields allow the prominences to hang in space.

■ HOW LONG DOES A PROMINENCE LAST?

Some last only a short time, but others may survive for several months. They are cooler than the Sun itself, and can form in a day or so.

■ WHAT SUPPORTS IT?

A prominence is held above the photosphere by powerful magnetic fields. However, we still do not really know why prominences form in the first place.

■ WHAT IS A CME?

CME is short for Coronal Mass Ejection, a billion-tonne cloud of electrified gas, blown off the Sun in a massive eruption.

CME
eruption

CME
eruption

WHAT'S ABOVE THE PHOTOSPHERE?

There are three layers to the Sun that we can see. The brightest but lowest layer is the photosphere. Just above this is the **chromosphere**, where **plages** occur. These are bright areas that usually form near sunspots. Above the chromosphere is the **corona**.

In other places over the surface, there are spicules. These are long, thin streamers of flame.

SO WHAT IS THE CORONA?

The corona is the Sun's outermost gas layer. It is thin but very hot, with temperatures that reach more than a million degrees.

Most of the corona's gases are trapped by magnetism above sunspots. In other places though, the corona passes far out into space.

■ From Earth, we can see the corona's pearly light when the Moon passes in front of the Sun during an eclipse (see page 24). At other times, the photosphere far outshines the corona, so it's visible only to astronomical instruments.

WOW!
CMEs are the most violent events we see on the Sun. During a CME, gas is blown into space at up to 2,000 kilometers a second!

■ The bright lights in this picture show Coronal Mass Ejections, or CMEs. During a CME, huge amounts of material are blown off the Sun and into space.
   Surprisingly, no one knew that these mega-events existed until the early 1970s, after instruments aboard the space observatory OSO-7 spotted a CME in progress.

DANGER IN SPACE?

The energy of CMEs and solar flares can interfere with radio and television, cause electricity blackouts, and even damage power lines.

Worse still, astronauts in space can be in danger, because CME energy can harm living tissue. So astronauts don't take spacewalks when a CME is expected!

■ WHAT IS THE SOLAR WIND?

The solar wind **is the constant stream of particles pouring out from the Sun, across the entire solar system.**

■ WHAT IS SPACE WEATHER?

It's the name for changing conditions in space, caused by varying energy patterns in the solar wind.

Luckily for us, the Earth's surface is largely protected from particles in the solar wind by the **magnetosphere**. This is a huge, natural magnetic shield that diverts much of the solar wind around our world.

■ The magnetosphere, shown in blue (arrowed), surrounds the Earth in a similar pattern to the iron filings around a bar magnet (see page 29). The magnetosphere diverts the solar wind around the Earth, protecting us from the deadliest particles.

Satellite picture shows the aurora surrounding Earth's North Pole

HOW DOES THE SOLAR WIND AFFECT THE EARTH?

The Northern and Southern Lights, or **auroras**, are caused by the Sun, though we see them only at night. The shifting patterns are caused when some solar wind particles hit the Earth's upper atmosphere. Energy from the impacts is given off as colored lights that we can see moving in the sky.

WHERE DOES THE WIND GO?

The solar wind covers a huge volume of space that goes beyond the planets, and is called the heliosphere.

Just as Earth's magnetosphere is shaped into a big bubble by the solar wind's pressure, so the heliosphere is shaped by particles coming from the Milky Way galaxy.

■ The auroras circle the North and South poles like glowing crowns. So, to see an aurora well, you need to be somewhere not too far from one of the poles. This photo was taken in the far north of the U.S.

■ Two Pioneer and two Voyager spacecraft are now exploring the outer edges of the heliosphere, after earlier flights past the outer planets.

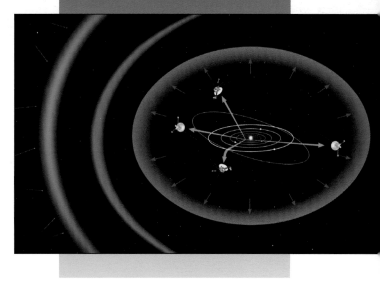

WHAT IS AN ECLIPSE?

A solar eclipse takes place when the Moon passes in front of the Sun, cutting off its light.

WHAT ARE TOTAL AND PARTIAL ECLIPSES?

Sometimes the Moon exactly covers the Sun, an event called a total eclipse. Much more often though, the Moon covers only a part of the Sun, when it is called a partial eclipse.

Sun

Moon moving in front of Sun

This series of photos shows the Moon passing in front of the Sun during a total eclipse. Early astronomers learned to predict eclipse dates with fair accuracy, more than 3,000 years ago. The long-range eclipse cycle is called a saros.

HOW LONG DOES AN ECLIPSE LAST?

Eclipses last for only a short time, because the Moon is always moving in its orbit around the Earth. Its shadow races across the world at 1,056 mph (1,700 km/h). At any point in this path, a total eclipse lasts little more than seven minutes.

It's rare to be directly in the path of a total eclipse, so scientists often travel a long way to be in just the right place. They sometimes fly in fast jet planes to keep up with the Moon's speeding shadow.

WOW!
Predicting solar eclipse times has not always been spot-on. In ancient China, astronomers were beheaded for getting the date wrong!

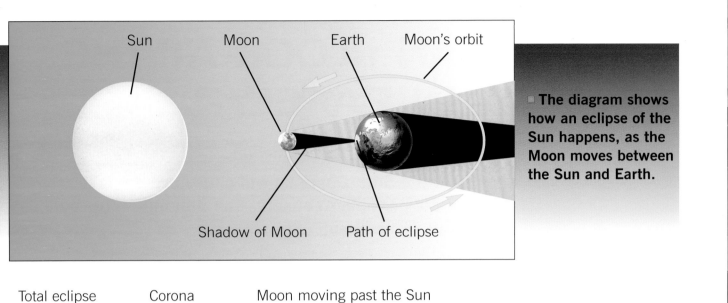

Sun   Moon   Earth   Moon's orbit

Shadow of Moon   Path of eclipse

■ **The diagram shows how an eclipse of the Sun happens, as the Moon moves between the Sun and Earth.**

Total eclipse   Corona   Moon moving past the Sun

■ WHAT IS THE DIAMOND RING EFFECT?

This picture shows what happens in the last few moments before a total eclipse, a period called totality. When the Sun goes behind the Moon, the corona starts to become visible.

Then, just before the Sun vanishes behind the Moon, the "diamond ring" effect comes into view for a few seconds. Then the effect vanishes, and the Sun's corona can be seen properly.

■ **The beautiful diamond ring effect lasts only a few moments.**

■ HOW CAN I LOOK AT THE SUN SAFELY?

NEVER look directly at the Sun. Doing so will cause eye damage, or blindness. However, it's possible to observe the Sun indirectly, by projecting its image onto a screen.

■ WHO WERE THE FIRST SOLAR ASTRONOMERS?

Many early peoples worshiped the Sun as part of their religion. Some built huge structures as temples, or perhaps observatories. Stonehenge in Britain (above) was built more than 4,000 years ago. The stones are laid out to mark the Sun's position at various times of year.

■ WHAT IS THE BIGGEST SOLAR TELESCOPE?

This is the huge McMath-Pierce telescope. It was built in 1962, at Kitt Peak in Arizona, U.S.

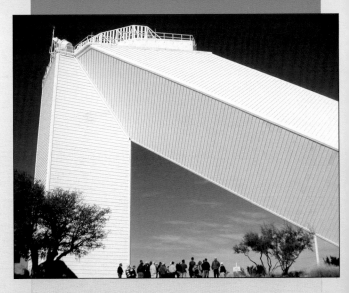

■ **The McMath-Pierce telescope has revolving mirrors that follow the Sun as it moves in the sky. Light is directed down this sloping shaft, where more mirrors reflect it to a viewing screen.**

Venus starts to pass in
front of the Sun

■ **This six-inch telescope was used to view a rare event, a transit of the planet Venus, when it passed between the Sun and the Earth. Venus is much further away from Earth than the Moon, so it appeared as a black dot, rather than blocking off the Sun entirely. It crossed the Sun in six hours.**

■ HOW CAN I SAFELY PROJECT THE SUN'S IMAGE?

Amateur astronomers can project the Sun's image by holding a flat sheet of card near the eyepiece of a small telescope. The eyepiece then projects the Sun's image onto the card, which acts as a viewing screen.

A pair of binoculars can do the same, if you cover one of the eyepieces with black tape. The important safety point is NEVER to look at the Sun while you aim the binoculars or telescope.

Venus moves
across the Sun

■ FACTS AND FIGURES

■ SOLAR STATISTICS

Diameter

865,000 miles (1,392,000 km), making the Sun 109 times wider than the Earth.

Time to rotate

25.2 days average. However, the Sun is not solid like the Earth, and its rotation time varies, from 34.4 days at the poles, to 25.1 days at the equator.

Distance from Earth

92.6 million miles (149 million km). The Sun's light takes 8.3 minutes to travel across space to the Earth.

Composition

The Sun is made up of 71 percent hydrogen, 27.1 percent helium, and less than 2 percent of other materials, including carbon, oxygen, nitrogen, and iron.

Temperature

The Sun's surface temperature is 9,930°F (5,500°C). Deep inside the Sun's core, temperatures may reach about 28 million°F (15.5 million°C).

Mass

The Sun contains some 99.8 percent of all matter in the solar system. It works out to nearly 333,000 times more than all the matter contained in the Earth.

Surface gravity

Here on Earth we live under a force of one **gravity**, or 1G. If you could stand on the photosphere, it would pull down on you with a force of 28G.

■ Sunlight is a free source of energy, which we can put to use with solar panels. These have silicon materials that change the energy in sunlight to electricity.

There is a huge amount of energy available from the Sun. If we could use it efficiently, there would be no shortage of energy on the Earth.

■ From being formed in a gas cloud sometime about 4.6 billion years ago, to its final end as a cold, dark cinder, the Sun's lifetime will have been roughly 12 billion years.

Sun today

Future Sun starts to warm up

Red giant

White dwarf

Today the Sun is in early middle age, pouring out a steady supply of heat and light. But long before it cools off, the Sun will start to swell and get hotter. Eventually, the Earth's seas and oceans will have boiled to steam, and even the rocks may have melted.

Travelling nonstop at 62 mph (100 km/hour) it would take about 170 years to reach the photosphere. Of course, in reality you would have been burnt to a crisp long before then!

■ FASCINATING FACTS

HOW MUCH FUEL DOES THE SUN USE IN ITS CORE?

In the Sun's core, materials are pressed together so hard that particles of hydrogen join together, or fuse, to make helium. Each time this process of nuclear fusion happens, a little matter is lost, and given off as energy. In this way, the Sun loses about 4 million tonnes of matter every second. Even so, because the Sun is so massive, it should continue to shine steadily for at least another 5 billion years.

Here on Earth, scientists are now trying to produce controlled fusion to make cheap and safe electricity in a power station.

HOW LONG WOULD IT TAKE TO REACH THE SUN?

An easy way to get a feel for the distance involved is to think of going on a car journey.

HOW FAST IS THE SOLAR WIND?

The solar wind does not move at any one speed. Typically, it blows past the Earth at about 1 million mph (1.6 million km/h), though it can gust to twice this speed.

■ Swirling gases inside the Sun create huge forces that make the Sun a giant natural magnet. Magnetic fields come from the Sun's poles, much like the patterns around an ordinary bar magnet.

■ GLOSSARY

Here are explanations for many of the terms used in this book.

Aurora Glowing curtains of light caused by the solar wind hitting Earth's atmosphere.

Chromosphere Part of the Sun's atmosphere, just above the photosphere.

CME Coronal Mass Ejection, material blown off the Sun's corona.

Convective zone Region inside the Sun where energy is taken up to the photosphere by streams of gases.

Core The center of the Sun, where energy is produced.

Corona The outer layer of the Sun's atmosphere, mainly gases trapped in magnetic fields.

Eclipse When part of the Sun (partial eclipse), or all of it (total eclipse) is hidden by the Moon passing in front.

Flare A sudden brightening on part of the Sun's surface, releasing energy into the solar wind.

Granulation The moving grainy pattern on the photosphere. Caused by gas cells rising to the surface, then sinking again, when their energy has been released.

■ **These are the eight planets that orbit the Sun.**

Gravity The universal force of attraction between all objects.

Helium Second lightest element, also the second major material in the Sun.

Hydrogen The commonest substance in the universe, also the most important part of the Sun's makeup.

Magnetic field The area of influence around anything that has magnetism.

Magnetosphere The magnetic field region around the Earth. It is shaped into a bubble by the pressure of the solar wind blowing against it.

Maunder Minimum A period of low sunspot activity, from 1645 to 1715.

Milky Way galaxy The huge spiral of stars to which our Sun belongs.

Nebula A cloud of gas and dust in outer space.

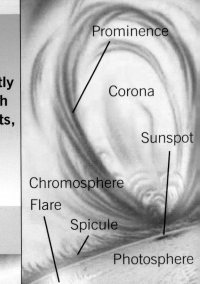

Prominence

Corona

Sunspot

Chromosphere

Flare

Spicule

Photosphere

■ **The Sun is constantly boiling with flares, spots, and other activity.**

Nuclear fusion The energy that powers the Sun. Caused by hydrogen fusing under immense pressure at the Sun's core to form helium, giving off energy in the process.

Orbit The curving path a space object takes around a more massive one. The Moon orbits the bigger Earth, as the Earth orbits the much bigger Sun.

Photosphere The visible, glowing surface of the Sun.

Plage A dense cloud of gases, usually found near sunspots.

Prominence Arch of gas hanging above the Sun, in the corona.

Radiative zone Region deep inside the Sun, where energy travels from the core to the outer convective zone.

Red giant A future stage of the Sun, when it will expand to become far bigger than it is today.

Satellite Any space object that orbits around a bigger one. It can be a natural satellite, such as the Moon, or a human-made one, such as the SOHO space observatory.

Solar cycle A period of about 11 years during which all solar activity, including sunspots and prominences, reaches a peak then dies away again. Also used just for the sunspot cycle.

Solar system Name for the Sun, planets and their moons, plus billions of rocks, and space dust.

Solar wind The stream of gases that pour from the Sun throughout the solar system.

Umbra The dark central part of a sunspot. The penumbra is lighter and surrounds the umbra.

White dwarf The small, hot, remains of a star such as the Sun, after its red giant period. Eventually, the white dwarf will cool off to become a cold, dark, black dwarf.

☐ Satellite picture of the Sun's surface. These loops of gas reach up into the corona.

■ GOING FURTHER

Using the Internet is a great way to expand your knowledge of the Sun and the solar system.

Your first port of call could be to the U.S. space agency, NASA. Its site shows almost everything to do with space, from the history of spaceflight to astronomy and plans for future space missions.

There are also news websites that give detailed reports on space. Try these sites to start with:

http://www.nasa.gov	Biggest and best!
http://www.spacedaily.com/	Good for headlines.
http://www.space.com	Lots of videos.
http://www.spaceweather.com	Immense detail.
http://www.astronomy.com	General interest.

■INDEX

Printed in the U.S.A.